American Biographies

GEORGE WASHINGTON

Casey Rand

Heinemann
LIBRARY

Chicago, Illinois

www.capstonepub.com
Visit our website to find out more information about Heinemann-Raintree books.

To order:
☎ Phone 800-747-4992
▣ Visit www.capstonepub.com to browse our catalog and order online.

Edited by Abby Colich, Megan Cotugno, and Laura Hensley
Designed by Philippa Jenkins
Original illustrations © Capstone Global Library Limited 2011
Illustrated by Oxford Designers and Illustrators
Picture research by Tracy Cummins
Originated by Capstone Global Library Limited
Printed and bound in China by Leo Paper Group

16 15 14 13 12
10 9 8 7 6 5 4 3 2 1

Library of Congress Cataloging-in-Publication Data
Rand, Casey.
  George Washington / Casey Rand.
    p. cm.—(American biographies)
  Includes bibliographical references and index.
  ISBN 978-1-4329-6452-8 (hb)—ISBN 978-1-4329-6463-4 (pb) 1. Washington, George, 1732-1799—Juvenile literature. 2. Presidents—United States—Biography—Juvenile literature. I. Title.
  E312.66.R35 2013
  973.4'1092—dc23   2011037576
  [B]

Acknowledgments
The author and publishers are grateful to the following for permission to reproduce copyright material: Alamy: pp. 32 (© North Wind Picture Archives), 38 (© North Wind Picture Archives); Corbis: pp. 6 (© Bettmann), 7 (© PoodlesRock), 10 (© PoodlesRock), 18 (© Bettmann), 26 (© Bettmann); Getty Images: pp. 14 (The Bridgeman Art Library), 34 (The Bridgeman Art Library), 36 (MPI); Library of Congress Prints & Photographs Division: pp. 12, 13, 16, 19, 20, 21, 22, 25, 28, 29, 30, 35; National Archive: p. 27; Shutterstock: pp. 4 (© Victorian Traditions), 23 (© Perennial Foodie Traveler), 33 (© Ken Schulze), 37 (© David Kay), 39 (© Joe Gough), 40 (© Francesco Dazzi), 41 (© somersault18:24); The Granger Collection, NYC: pp. 17, 24.

Cover image of George Washington at Princeton reproduced with permission from Getty Images (Charles P. Polk and Charles W. Peale).

Every effort has been made to contact copyright holders of material reproduced in this book. Any omissions will be rectified in subsequent printings if notice is given to the publisher.

Disclaimer
All the Internet addresses (URLs) given in this book were valid at the time of going to press. However, due to the dynamic nature of the Internet, some addresses may have changed, or sites may have changed or ceased to exist since publication. While the author and publisher regret any inconvenience this may cause readers, no responsibility for any such changes can be accepted by either the author or the publisher.

Contents

Some words are shown in bold, **like this**.
These words are explained in the glossary.

George Washington: Father of the United States

George Washington lived from 1732 to 1799. He played a big role in forming and shaping the United States—as a military commander, as a politician, and as a leader.

George Washington played an important role in helping free the American colonies from British rule.

Military man

The United States was first formed from 13 separate **colonies** (see the map on page 8). These colonies were under the rule of Great Britain for most of the 1600s and 1700s. However, in the 1770s, the American **colonists** decided that they wanted to join together and form their own country, without British rule.

At this time, George Washington was considered the top military man in all of the land. So when the colonies formed a military, they put him in command. Washington led this army in the war to free the colonies from British rule. He fought for many years and eventually won.

President

After the war, George Washington was very famous and respected. The new country needed a leader, and everyone thought Washington was the perfect choice. He was elected the first president of the United States, serving from 1789 to 1797.

Did you know?

The men who had important roles in helping the United States become a country are often called the **Founding Fathers**. George Washington was just one of the Founding Fathers, but people often call him the Father of the Country because he played so many different important roles in shaping the nation.

Preparing to Lead

George Washington was not born a great leader. He had many experiences that helped him develop the skills needed to become the father of the United States.

Working as a surveyor helped George Washington learn skills to survive in the wilderness.

George was born in Virginia in 1732. He grew up on a farm his family owned, and he had nine brothers and sisters. On the farm, George learned to ride horses, hunt, and fish. He only went to school for about seven or eight years. When George was 11 years old, his father died, so George helped his mother run the farm.

First job

When George was 15 years old, he began working as a **surveyor**. A surveyor is a person who measures land and makes maps. George liked this job because it let him travel and see much of the country.

Fact VS. Fiction

You may have heard that when George Washington was a boy, he tried his new **hatchet** on a cherry tree and killed the tree. The story goes that his father was angry when he saw the tree and asked George if he knew what had happened. George is said to have responded, "I can't tell a lie, Pa; you know I can't tell a lie. I cut it with my hatchet." His father was proud of George for telling the truth. While this is a good story, it is probably not true. A writer named Mason Weems wrote this story, and many historians believe he made it up.

The story of George Washington and the cherry tree is probably not true.

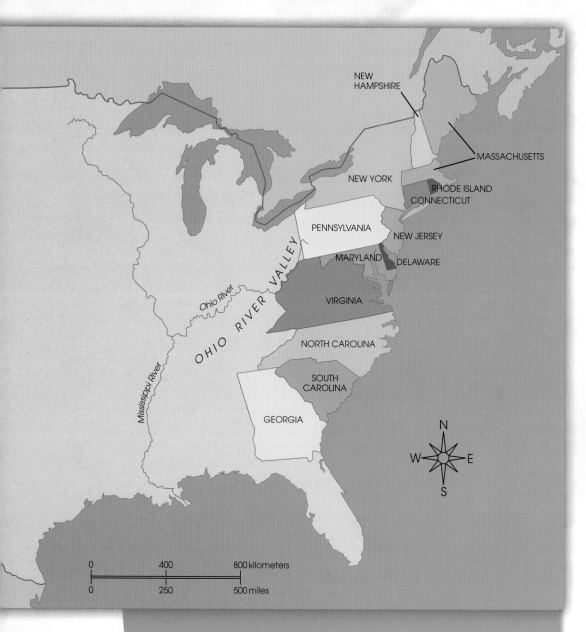

NEW
HAMPSHIRE

MASSACHUSETTS

NEW YORK

RHODE ISLAND
CONNECTICUT

PENNSYLVANIA

NEW JERSEY

MARYLAND

DELAWARE

VIRGINIA

NORTH CAROLINA

SOUTH
CAROLINA

GEORGIA

Ohio River

OHIO RIVER VALLEY

Mississippi River

N
W   E
S

| 0 | 400 | 800 kilometers |
| 0 | 250 | 500 miles |

These are the 13 original colonies in what is
now the United States. In the 1750s, the British
controlled the 13 colonies. The Ohio River Valley
was less developed, and the French, British, and
groups of American Indians all wanted to use
this land for themselves.

Mounting tensions

When George Washington was 21 years old, he joined the Virginia Army. Virginia was one of the 13 original **colonies** that would eventually join together to form the United States.

During the mid-1700s, the French were building settlements and forts in the Ohio River Valley region (see the map). The British did not like this. Both the British and the French thought the Ohio River Valley belonged to their country.

Courage under fire

The British wanted to send a message to the French, to tell them to stop building in the Ohio River Valley. They needed someone to deliver this message. Almost everyone in the army was too afraid to take this job, but Washington wanted the job. He volunteered to carry the message from the British to a French fort in the Ohio River Valley.

Battle begins

When Washington delivered the message to the French, they told him they would not stop building in the Ohio River Valley. When Washington returned to Virginia, the British governor sent him back with soldiers to repeat the message to the French. Along the way, Washington and his soldiers met up with some French soldiers and began to fight. This was the start of what is known as the **French and Indian War**.

Different tribes of American Indians fought on either the British or French sides in the French and Indian War.

Worldwide war

The French and Indian War began in 1754 in North America. A few years later, the war erupted into a worldwide conflict, which became known as the Seven Years' War. This war was fought across much of Europe and the Americas.

As a British **colonist**, Washington fought on the side of the British Army during these years. He became widely admired for his bravery and leadership. He did not know that later he would fight against the British.

Washington in battle

The British sent Washington on missions to try to take the French-held Fort Duquesne, located in present-day Pennsylvania, three different times. All three of these missions failed. But Washington survived each mission, and he became a well-known and respected soldier.

Washington assisted the British general Edward Braddock in one of these missions, and he copied many of his commands into a diary. Even when he lost, Washington was learning a great deal about how to lead an army into battle.

Eventually the British won the French and Indian War. By fighting alongside the British Army, Washington had learned the strengths and weaknesses of the British.

Did you know?

In 1755 Washington and the troops he was fighting with were badly defeated by the French at Monongahela, in present-day Pennsylvania. After the battle, Washington sent a letter to his mother. He told her that during the battle he "had four bullets through my coat, and two horses shot under me." This battle was a close call for Washington, but somehow he made it out unharmed.

11

Peace and Planning

After Washington resigned from the **French and Indian War**, he returned home to Virginia to tend to his farm and start a family. His family farm was called Mount Vernon, and he was glad to be home. The war had made him tired and ill. But Washington was a famous and respected man now. His country would soon need him again.

The Washingtons loved to spend time at their home, Mount Vernon.

Politics

In 1758 Washington was elected to join the part of the Virginia government called the House of Burgesses. Here he helped create laws and settle disputes, or arguments. Washington served many years in this role, learning how to deal with government and politics.

Love and marriage

In 1759 George Washington married Martha Custis. The couple lived many happy years together. Washington never had children of his own. But when he married Martha, she already had two children from a previous marriage (her husband had died). Washington treated these children as his own, and they all lived together at Mount Vernon.

Martha Washington
(1731–1802)

Born in Virginia, Martha Washington grew up learning to sew, cook, and manage a household. Once she moved to Mount Vernon with George, she began private music lessons. She loved being at Mount Vernon with her husband. But she would have to give up much of her time with him as he served his country. Still, Martha supported George and visited him whenever possible when he was away.

George and Martha Washington were married for 40 years.

The Boston Tea Party was one of the first major acts of revolt by the American colonists against British rule.

Melting pot

During the 1700s, the 13 **colonies** were already becoming a "melting pot" of people. This means there were many different kinds of people living in the same places and sharing their **cultures**. There were people of English, Irish, American Indian, Swedish, Welsh, German, French, and African descent (background). While the cultures and lifestyles of these people were all different, they each influenced the others. The colonies were beginning to feel more and more separate from Great Britain.

Taxation without representation

During the 1760s, many **colonists** began to get tired of British rule. These American colonists had to pay taxes to the British government, but they were not represented in the British government.

In the early 1770s, the British decided to tax the colonists even more, creating special taxes on tea that was brought into the colonies. Colonists felt the taxes were extremely unfair. They decided that they wanted their independence from Great Britain and they were going to fight for it.

Boston Tea Party

On December 16, 1773, colonists in the city of Boston refused to pay the new British tax on tea. Three ships filled with tea had been sent to Boston. The colonists refused to accept the tea. The British refused to send it back. In protest, the colonists climbed aboard the ships and threw all of the tea into Boston Harbor. This event became known as the Boston Tea Party.

Continental Congress

After the Boston Tea Party, the colonists decided they needed to figure out what to do about the British taxes and rule. Twelve of the colonies elected men to go to Philadelphia, Pennsylvania, to meet and discuss these issues. This meeting would be known as the First **Continental Congress**. George Washington was one of the men elected to represent Virginia at the meeting.

Washington and the other men at the Continental Congress wanted to show the British that they would not tolerate harsh laws and unfair treatment. But many of them disagreed on how to do this. Some colonists wanted to work things out with the British and avoid war. Others wanted to govern themselves. The men debated for weeks. Finally, they came up with a list of requests to send to the British king, George III.

British soldiers were often called redcoats, because of their uniforms. Many redcoats were sent to the colonies after the First Continental Congress.

"The redcoats are coming!"

After reading the requests of the first Continental Congress, King George III declared that the colonies were in rebellion. He said that the members of the Continental Congress were all **traitors**. The king decided to send troops into the colonies to stop the rebellion and arrest the traitors.

The First Continental Congress took place at Carpenter's Hall in Philadelphia in September 1774.

Fact VS. Fiction

At the time of the First Continental Congress, many men wore wigs. Some people think Washington wore a wig as well. But this is fiction. Washington did not wear a wig. He did powder his hair, to make it look white, but he did not wear a wig.

Revolutionary War

The British king, George III, sent troops into the American **colonies**. He probably expected a quick end to the revolt. He did not think the **colonists** would fight back. But he was wrong.

Paul Revere rode on horseback from Boston to Lexington to warn people British troops were coming.

Militia

While the 13 colonies did not have a formal military, they did have **militias**. These were groups of soldiers normally used to protect their people and land from invasion by American Indians. Some of these men had fought in the **French and Indian War** on the side of the British. Now they were preparing to fight against the British. Compared to the British Army, the militias were not well trained or well organized.

The "shot heard 'round the world"

In April 1775, British troops were sent from Boston to destroy rebel military stores at Concord and to capture Samuel Adams and John Hancock. Colonists from Boston, including Paul Revere, rode on horseback to warn the other colonists.

The militia got ready to confront the British troops. About 77 militiamen confronted a group of 700 British soldiers in Lexington, Massachusetts. Shots were fired. A few militiamen were killed, and the British marched on toward Concord, Massachusetts. However, more militiamen gathered and fiercely attacked the British troops. The British retreated and lost many soldiers along the way. These battles, known as the Battles of Lexington and Concord, were the first fighting of the **Revolutionary War**.

The first shot fired at Lexington was the start of the Revolutionary War. It is known as the "shot heard 'round the world."

Commanding the troops

After the Battles of Lexington and Concord, the members of the **Continental Congress** knew they needed a plan. They met again on May 10, 1775, in Philadelphia. They made a plan to officially unite and to create a united army. They also chose George Washington to lead this army.

But most of the members of the Continental Congress did not want war. They asked King George III to find a peaceful way to settle their differences. The king refused, and instead he paid German **mercenary** soldiers to bring the colonies under control.

During the Revolutionary War, the winters were cold, and the soldiers often did not have enough boots, coats, blankets, or shelter.

The fight for freedom

For much of the war, Washington and his troops were losing more battles than they were winning. The British troops were better organized and trained than Washington's army. Both sides had to battle the cold winters of the war, sometimes without food or shelter.

After Washington crossed the Delaware River, the German mercenaries surrendered without a fight.

The mighty Delaware

Washington decided that he needed a big victory to turn the tide of the war. He decided to make a daring attack across a large river called the Delaware. And he decided he should make the attack on Christmas night in 1776.

The attack worked! Washington and his troops surprised the German mercenaries across the river in Trenton, New Jersey. The mercenaries were celebrating Christmas and were not prepared to fight. This would become a turning point in the war.

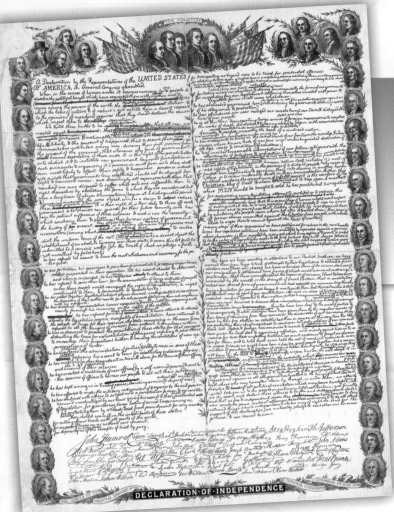

The Declaration of Independence was written by Thomas Jefferson and other members of the Continental Congress.

Fact VS. Fiction

Some people think that Washington helped write the Declaration of Independence, but he didn't. While the Declaration was being written, Washington was with his troops. Shortly after it was written, John Hancock sent Washington a copy of the Declaration of Independence to share with the troops.

Declaring independence

On July 4, 1776, the members of the Continental Congress approved the **Declaration of Independence**. This was a document to tell the world that the 13 colonies were forming their own, independent government. It also explained why they wanted separation from Great Britain.

Power of the pen

The Declaration of Independence had a powerful effect. It motivated the people and troops in the fight for independence. It also had a lasting effect on life in the United States long after the Revolutionary War. The declaration contains the following sentence, which is one of the most recognizable and influential sentences ever written:

> "We hold these truths to be self-evident, that all men are created equal, that they are endowed by their Creator with certain unalienable Rights, that among these are Life, Liberty and the pursuit of Happiness."

France gave the Statue of Liberty to the United States as a gift in 1886.

Did you know?

The Statue of Liberty is a large statue located in New York Harbor, off New York City. It shows the Roman goddess of freedom. The figure holds a tablet, on which is carved the date of the Declaration of Independence.

Friends in the fight

The American colonies were not alone in their war against Great Britain. France and Spain were two of the most powerful countries in the world at this time, and they did not like Britain very much. This would help the colonists in their war.

France and the United States signed a **treaty** in 1778. This meant the French would help the North American colonists fight against Great Britain. In 1779 Spain declared war on Great Britain as well. Having these countries as additional enemies affected the ability of the British military to focus its troops on the United States, which greatly helped the cause of the colonists.

William Lee
(c.1750–1828)

William Lee was a black slave and the personal servant of George Washington throughout the Revolutionary War. He rode with Washington in many battles, risking his life for Washington. Because of his loyal service, Washington had great respect for Lee. When Washington died, he freed Lee from **slavery**, citing "his faithful services during the Revolutionary War." He also gave Lee a retirement **pension** for the rest of his life. Although Lee was free to leave Mount Vernon, he chose to stay and live out the rest of his days with the Washington family.

William Lee fought in many battles with Washington during the Revolutionary War.

Soon after the surrender of General Cornwallis at Yorktown, the United States became an independent nation.

Victory

In October 1781, with the help of the French, Washington and his army forced a large part of the British Army in America to surrender. American and French forces trapped the British in Yorktown, Virginia. General Charles Cornwallis, commander of the British forces, had no choice but to give up. The United States would soon have its independence.

A New Nation

After the war ended, the United States officially became a self-governing nation. Washington was ready to return home to Mount Vernon and retire to family life and rest.

But the new country was taking shape, and the people of the United States needed leadership and guidance. There would be no rest for Washington. His leadership during the war was only the beginning.

Washington and the Constitutional Convention helped shape the future of the new nation.

Planning for democracy

The United States was free from British rule and had to create its own government. During the Second **Continental Congress**, a document called the **Articles of Confederation** had been created to guide the new government. But this document had left the **federal** government of the United States very weak and unable to efficiently govern the states. A new plan was needed. In 1787 the **Constitutional Convention** met in Philadelphia to create a new plan. Washington was elected by the members to lead the convention.

The Constitution of the United States is considered the supreme law of the land.

Writing the Constitution

Representatives from 12 of the states came to the convention, each with their own ideas about how things should be run. The federal government needed more power, but nobody knew exactly how much to give it. It had to be powerful enough to govern effectively, but the members of the convention did not want another king. The members of the convention had to cooperate and compromise in order to create the new plan.

This new plan was called the **Constitution** of the United States. It is the document the United States government is still based on today.

George Washington became the first president of the United States in 1789.

Did you know?

George Washington was the only president ever to be unanimously elected.

Fit to be king

The Constitution created a plan for a stronger federal government, which would be led by an elected official called the president. This person would not be an all-powerful king, but would be the leader of the country. In 1789 the **electors** representing the states **unanimously** voted for George Washington to become the first president of the United States.

There were many reasons people thought Washington should be the president:

- Washington had successfully led the military against the British.
- Washington had turned down a chance to be king after the war, because he thought the new ruler should be elected.
- Washington had led the Constitutional Convention, creating the plan for the new government.

Now Washington would be the country's first president, the man in charge of putting forward the new plan. Although Washington was ready to retire, he could not turn down the great honor, and so he accepted the position.

John Adams

(1735–1826)

John Adams was one of the most influential **Founding Fathers**. He was a member of the Continental Congress and one of the writers of the **Declaration of Independence**, and he nominated George Washington to become commander in chief of the army. Adams would later serve two terms as the vice president under Washington. He eventually became the second president of the United States (1797–1801).

John Adams was the second president of the United States. His son John Quincy Adams would later become the sixth president.

The Presidency

As the first president of the United States, Washington knew he had a lot of work to do. The new nation would need strong leadership as people worked to form the new government and make it operate.

Independence Hall in Philadelphia had served as the meeting place of the Second **Continental Congress** and the **Constitutional Convention.** But after 1791 the new center of government would be Washington, D.C.

A new capital

Philadelphia was the site where the **Founding Fathers** had gathered, and it was considered the first capital of the United States. But the **Constitution** had made plans for a self-governing district to become the capital of the new U.S. government. This meant that the **federal** government would not be located in any particular state, to be fair to all of the states. In 1791 Congress established the District of Columbia. This district would be the site of the U.S. federal government.

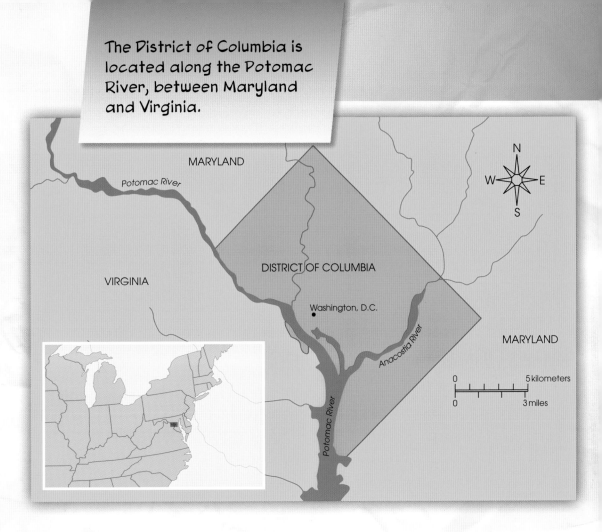

The District of Columbia is located along the Potomac River, between Maryland and Virginia.

MARYLAND

Potomac River

VIRGINIA

DISTRICT OF COLUMBIA

Washington, D.C.

MARYLAND

Anacostia River

Potomac River

0   5 kilometers

0   3 miles

N
W   E
S

Bill of Rights

Soon after the Constitution was created, it needed to be changed. Things were changing every day, and President Washington and others realized that the Constitution would have to change with it.

Washington worked with Congress to come up with a list of **amendments** to be made to the Constitution. The first 10 amendments to the Constitution guarantee basic **liberties** to Americans. They include freedom of religion, speech, and press, as well as the right to bear arms (have firearms, or guns). They were meant to limit the power of the federal government and guarantee the rights of individual people. These 10 amendments became knows as the **Bill of Rights**. They became law in 1791.

31

Whiskey Rebellion

In 1792 Washington was elected to a second term as president. While he had worked to limit the power of the federal government, he also needed to show the states that the president—and the federal government—could be powerful if needed.

In 1794 a large group of farmers in Pennsylvania refused to pay federal taxes on whiskey they had made. These farmers had guns and even attacked some federal officials who were trying to collect taxes. This became known as the Whiskey Rebellion. Washington sent in thousands of troops to stop the rebellion and to make the farmers pay their taxes. This was the first real show of power by the federal government.

During the Whiskey Rebellion, Washington let the states know that the federal government would not be pushed around.

Did you know?

During his time as president, Washington helped to establish both the federal bank and the U.S. Mint (the place that produces and distributes coins). Washington made such an impact on the banking industry of the United States that his face appears on two of the most used forms of money in the country—the dollar bill and the quarter.

George Washington appears on both the quarter and the dollar bill.

Fact VS. Fiction

You may have heard that George Washington had teeth made of wood. This is actually not true. Washington did have false teeth, but they were not made of wood. His dentist used cows' teeth and hippopotamus ivory to make false teeth for Washington. This is why Washington never appears to be smiling in any of his pictures.

Washington was determined to keep the United States out of the French Revolution and other bloody conflicts.

A changing world

During Washington's time as president (1789–1797), the United States and the world were changing quickly. The **French Revolution** (1789–1799) began, in which the French king was overthrown. In addition, France and Great Britain were at war once again.

Peacemaker

Washington was determined to stay out of conflict. In 1793 he issued a Proclamation of Neutrality to keep the United States out of the war between France and Great Britain. ("Neutrality" means not choosing a side.)

In 1795 Washington signed a document called the Jay **Treaty**, which maintained trade with Great Britain. Many American people did not like this treaty. But it made relations with Great Britain stable and avoided conflict. Washington's skills as a politician helped him successfully avoid many conflicts during his presidency.

Changing leadership

When Washington had served two terms as president, he was ready to go home. Although the people wanted him to return for a third term, Washington refused. This set the stage for nonviolent transfers of power in the United States, which has been the case ever since.

King George III

(1738–1820)

King George III was king of Great Britain from 1760 until his death in 1820. He was considered Washington's opponent. When King George III heard that Washington wanted to retire to his farm, leaving behind all of his power, the king replied: "If he does that, he will be the greatest man in the world." Perhaps the king was right.

King George III was the leader of Great Britain during the **Revolutionary War.**

Life in Retirement

Finally, Washington could retire to his home at Mount Vernon. He loved his farm and wanted to spend time with Martha again. He loved to ride horses, and now he could ride across his farm each day to oversee the work. Washington also loved making maps. Even in retirement Washington had a lot of plans and things to do.

In retirement, Washington enjoyed riding his horse every day.

Ready and willing

Washington lived the life of retirement for only a short time before duty called again. The **French Revolution** had removed the French king from power, leaving the government there a mess. Relations between the new French government and the United States were deteriorating (falling apart). In 1798 John Adams, the new U.S. president, asked Washington to be ready to lead the troops again if war came. Washington reluctantly accepted the position. Fortunately, President Adams was able to negotiate, and war was avoided.

Washington, D.C.

After the District of Columbia was chosen as the location of the new U.S. government, construction began on the government buildings that would be located there. In retirement, Washington would sometimes ride his horse 15 miles (24 kilometers) to check on the progress of the buildings in the capital.

In 1791 the United States named its capital city Washington, D.C., to honor George Washington.

The end of an era

Like most landowners of his time, Washington owned many slaves.

Late in 1799, Washington became ill after a day riding his horse in freezing rain and snow. Washington died of a throat infection a few days later, on December 14, 1799. He was 67 years old.

Washington's will and slavery

Washington was from a wealthy family. He owned a large number of slaves. As Washington grew older, his beliefs about **slavery** changed. There were thousands of African American men—both free and slaves—who had bravely fought under Washington during the **Revolutionary War.** William Lee (see page 24) had served Washington for many years and became a friend. In his **will**, Washington said that the hundreds of slaves he owned would be freed after Martha's death. He also left money to take care of many of his slaves for years after his death.

To this day, an empty tomb made for George Washington remains in the U.S. Capitol Building.

Fact VS. Fiction

You may have heard that George Washington is buried in the Capitol Building in Washington, D.C. This is fiction. Congress did have a tomb built for this purpose, but Washington wanted to be buried at Mount Vernon. The tomb at the Capitol Building has remained empty to this day.

A Nation Continues

George Washington is known as the "father" of the United States. He was truly a crucial figure in the development of the United States. Without his presence, the country may never have existed.

Former U.S. presidents (left to right) George Washington, Thomas Jefferson, Theodore Roosevelt, and Abraham Lincoln are honored by Mount Rushmore.

Did you know?

Carved into the stone of Mount Rushmore in Keystone, South Dakota, is a national memorial honoring George Washington and three other U.S. presidents. It is a giant sculpture that stands 60 feet (18 meters) tall. The entire memorial covers more than 1,200 acres (486 hectares) of rock. Construction began on the memorial in 1927, and it was completed in 1941.

In the **Continental Congress**, George Washington helped plan and shape the documents on which the nation would be based. He led the fight against the British king, George III, for independence during the **Revolutionary War**. He guided the members of the **Constitutional Convention** in shaping the **Constitution** of the United States. He took on the challenge of becoming the first president, and he helped steer the path of the new nation.

Honoring the father of the United States

The United States has found many ways to honor everything George Washington did for the country, including:

- using his image on the quarter
- using his image on the dollar bill
- naming the national capital Washington, D.C.
- naming Washington state after him
- naming 33 counties throughout the country "Washington"
- naming many cities throughout the country "Washington"
- building the Washington Monument in Washington, D.C.
- building Mount Rushmore (see the box).

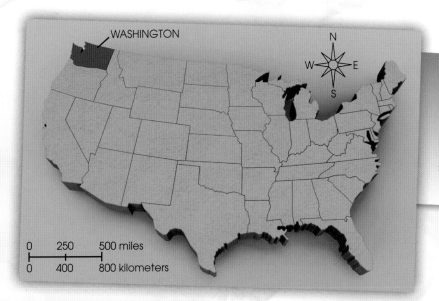

The state of Washington became the 42nd U.S. state in 1889.

Timeline

1732
George Washington is born in Westmoreland County, Virginia.

1749
Washington becomes a surveyor for Culpeper County, Virginia.

1753
Washington carries an order from the British to the French, telling them to stop building in the Ohio River Valley.

1789
Washington is elected the first president of the United States.

1787
Washington is elected president of the Constitutional Convention.

1781
The British surrender at Yorktown, Virginia.

1791
Congress establishes the District of Columbia, to become the new capital.

1791
The Bill of Rights becomes law.

1799
Washington dies of throat infection at Mount Vernon, at the age of 67.

1798
Washington prepares to lead troops into battle against France if needed, but no conflict begins.

1796
Washington publishes his Farewell Address, refusing a third term as president.

1754–1755

Washington fights in the French and Indian War.

1759

Washington marries Martha Custis.

1774

Washington is elected to the First Continental Congress.

1775

The Revolutionary War begins.

1775

Washington is elected commander in chief of the army representing the American colonists, called the Continental Army.

1775

Washington is elected to the Second Continental Congress.

1792

Washington is elected president for a second term.

1793

Washington issues the Proclamation of Neutrality to keep the United States out of the war between France and Great Britain.

1795

Washington signs the unpopular Jay Treaty to maintain trade with Great Britain.

1794

During the Whiskey Rebellion, Washington sends troops to crush an uprising by Pennsylvania farmers who refuse to pay a federal whiskey tax.

Glossary

amendment change to a law

Articles of Confederation document that was the first constitution before the current U.S. Constitution was written

Bill of Rights first 10 amendments of the U.S. Constitution, which guarantee liberties and rights to the people

colonist person who lives in a colony

colony place that has been settled by people from another country

Constitution U.S. document that lists the beliefs, laws, rights, and duties of the government and its people

Constitutional Convention meeting in 1787 to discuss plans to fix the problems the new U.S. government faced under the Articles of Confederation

Continental Congress meeting of representatives that first took place in Philadelphia in 1774 to discuss plans for the colonies to deal with the British government

culture shared beliefs, traditions, and behaviors belonging to a certain group of people

Declaration of Independence document created at the Constitutional Convention declaring the independence of the North American colonies from British rule

elector person who represents other people when voting in an election

federal central government authority

Founding Fathers group of men responsible for helping to liberate the American colonies from British rule and for designing plans for the new U.S. government

French and Indian War war fought from 1754 to 1763 between the British and the French for rights to land in the Americas, with certain tribes of American Indians joining either side of the struggle

French Revolution violent struggle in France from 1789 to 1799, when the French king was overthrown

hatchet small, short-handled ax

mercenary soldier hired by a foreign country to fight in its army

militia army made up of regular citizens, as opposed to professional soldiers

pension money paid to a retired person

Revolutionary War war fought between 1775 and 1783 in which the American colonies fought for independence from Great Britain

slavery relationship in which one person has absolute power over another and controls his or her life, liberty, and fortune

surveyor person who makes maps and measures land

traitor one who betrays another's trust

treaty agreement made by a negotiation

unanimous agreed to by all

will document with instructions for what happens to a person's property and belongings after death

Find Out More

Books

Allen, Thomas B. *George Washington, Spymaster: How the Americans Outspied the British and Won the Revolutionary War.* Washington, D.C.: National Geographic, 2007.

Calkhoven, Laurie. *George Washington: An American Life (Sterling Biographies).* New York: Sterling, 2007.

Edwards, Roberta. *Who Was George Washington?* New York: Grosset and Dunlap, 2009.

Murphy, Jim. *The Crossing: How George Washington Saved The American Revolution.* New York: Scholastic, 2010.

Pingry, Patricia A. *Meet George Washington.* Danbury, Conn.: Ideals, 2009.

DVDs

American Experience: George Washington: Man Who Wouldn't Be King. PBS, 2011.

Biography: George Washington—American Revolutionary. A&E Home Video, 2009.

The History Channel Presents Washington the Warrior. A&E Home Video, 2006.

Inspiring Animated Heroes: George Washington. Nest Family Entertainment, 2009.

Websites

George Washington: A National Treasure
www.georgewashington.si.edu/index.html
This is an interactive site with fun facts and information about George Washington.

George Washington's World for Kids
www.washingtonsworld.org
This fun site has games and trivia all about George Washington.

George Washington: The White House
www.whitehouse.gov/about/presidents/georgewashington
Read about all of the presidents at the White House's website.

Places to visit

George Washington Birthplace
1732 Popes Creek Road
Washington's Birthplace, VA 22443
804-224-1732
www.nps.gov/gewa/index.htm

Minutemen National Historical Park
174 Liberty Street
Concord, MA 01742
978-369-6993
www.nps.gov/mima/index.htm

Mount Rushmore
13000 Hwy 244 Bldg. 31 Suite 1
Keystone, SD 57751
605-574-2523
www.nps.gov/moru/index.htm

Mount Vernon
3200 Mount Vernon Memorial Highway
Mount Vernon, VA 22309
703-780-2000
www.mountvernon.org/

Washington Monument
900 Ohio Drive SW
Washington, DC 20024
202-426-6841
www.nps.gov/wamo/index.htm

Index